THEY DON'T **BELONG** TRACKING INVASIVE SPECIES

Guam's Brown Tree Snakes
Hanging Out

by Kevin Blake

Consultant: Gordon Rodda, PhD
Research Zoologist
Hesperus, CO

BEARPORT
PUBLISHING

New York, New York

Credits

Cover and Title Page, © Janelle Lugge/Shutterstock and © Evgeniya Uvarova/Shutterstock; 4T, © IZO/ Shutterstock; 4B, © U.S. Department of Agriculture/tinyurl.com/nf45m63/CC-BY-2.0; 5L, © iStockphoto/ michaklootwijk; 5R, © XNR Productions, Inc.; 6, © Bjorn Lardner; 7, © Janelle Lugge/Shutterstock; 8, © XNR Productions, Inc.; 9T, © Bettmann/Corbis/AP Images; 9B, © National Geographic Image Collection/Alamy; 10, © Ch'ien Lee/Getty Images; 11T, © IZO/Shutterstock; 11B, © Keith Tarrier/Shutterstock; 12, © Bjorn Lardner; 13T, © iStockphoto/aussiesnakes; 13B, © Kate Jackson; 14L, © Roland Seitre/naturepl; 14R, Nottsexminer/tinyurl. com/mg9adlj/CC-BY-SA 2.0; 15T, Chris Brown/USGS; 15B, USFWS-Pacific Region/tinyurl.com/lgq47lf/CC- BY-2.0; 16, © IZO/Shutterstock; 17T, © iStockphoto/OGphoto; 17B, Making-Things-Better/tinyurl.com/k2hsh9h/ CC-BY-ND-2.0; 18, © Gordon Rodda; 19T, U.S. Department of Agriculture/tinyurl.com/ohbwkbr/CC-BY-2.0; 19B, © iStockphoto/YinYang; 20, U.S. Department of Agriculture/tinyurl.com/loymmso/CC-BY-2.0; 21, U.S. Department of Agriculture/tinyurl.com/od3zpxr/CC-BY-2.0; 22, © AP Photo/Masako Watanabe-Pacific Daily News; 23, © MOLPIX/Shutterstock; 24, © Ammit Jack/Shutterstock; 25, U.S. Department of Agriculture/tinyurl. com/oa4dwcf/CC-BY-2.0; 26T, © Michael Warwick/Shutterstock; 26B, © zixian/iStock; 27, © iStockphoto/ MoMorad; 28T, Bjørn Christian Tørrissen/tinyurl.com/ppz8jc3/CC-BY-SA-3.0; 28B, Susan Jewell/USFWS/tinyurl. com/kx7wm5o/CC-BY-2.0; 29T, Cayambe/tinyurl.com/o4bwo5a/CC-BY-SA-3.0; 29B, D. Gordon E. Robertson/ tinyurl.com/megtrdl/CC-BY-SA-3.0.

Publisher: Kenn Goin
Senior Editor: Joyce Tavolacci
Creative Director: Spencer Brinker
Design: Dawn Beard Creative
Photo Researcher: Josh Gregory

Library of Congress Cataloging-in-Publication Data

Blake, Kevin, 1978– author.
  Guam's brown tree snakes : hanging out / by Kevin Blake.
    pages cm. — (They don't belong)
  Audience: Ages 7–12
  Includes bibliographical references and index.
  ISBN 978-1-62724-830-3 (library binding) — ISBN 1-62724-830-7 (library binding)
 1. Brown tree snake—Guam—Juvenile literature. 2. Pest introduction—Guam—Juvenile literature. 3. Nonindigenous pests—Guam—Juvenile literature. 4. Nature—Effect of human beings on—Juvenile literature. I. Title. II. Title: Brown tree snakes.
  QL666.O636B53 2016
  597.96'2—dc23
                                   2015008516

For more information, write to Bearport Publishing Company, Inc., 45 West 21st Street, Suite 3B, New York, New York 10010. Printed in the United States of America.

10 9 8 7 6 5 4 3 2 1

Contents

Operation Mouse

It's December 2013. A helicopter **hovers** above a thick patch of trees on the **tropical** island of Guam (GWAHM). A scientist slides open the chopper's side door. He grabs a handful of dead mice that have been stuffed with a special kind of poison. Then he tosses them out the door.

mouse

Scientists scatter the mice among the treetops.

A dead mouse

Once the mice are in the air, small **parachutes** attached to the tiny animals pop open. The mice float down, land on trees, and then dangle from their branches. The mice will soon become a **toxic** meal for Guam's number one enemy: the hungry brown tree snake!

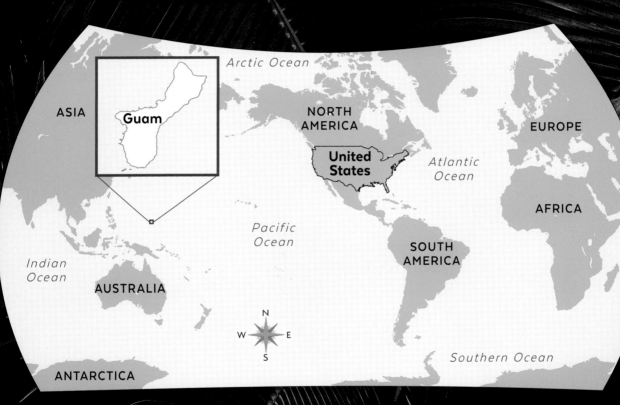

Guam is a tiny island in the Pacific Ocean that's part of the United States. It's 212 square miles (549 sq km) in area—about three times as big as Washington, DC.

The dead mice were stuffed with medicine that people use as a common pain reliever. This medicine is deadly to brown tree snakes but usually not to other animals on Guam.

Millions of Problems

Why would scientists throw poison-filled mice into the trees of Guam? The mice are just their latest attempt to control the **population** of **invasive** brown tree snakes.

A brown snake coils its body around a dead mouse.

The brown tree snake is brown, with a yellow or cream-colored belly.

About one million snakes live on the island. They hang from the trees, slither on the ground, and hide in people's homes. The snakes are more than just pests. In fact, they cause major problems for the animals, plants, and people of Guam. Each day, as more snakes are born and spread to new areas, the problem gets worse and worse.

Brown tree snakes prefer to live high in the treetops.

Arriving in Guam

Just 80 years ago, there were no brown tree snakes on Guam. That's because the snakes aren't **native** to the island. The **reptiles** are originally from Papua New Guinea, Indonesia, and Australia. In their homelands, the snakes aren't considered pests. There, **predators** such as wild pigs and large lizards hunt them. Also, there isn't a lot of food for the snakes to eat. As a result, their numbers never grow too large.

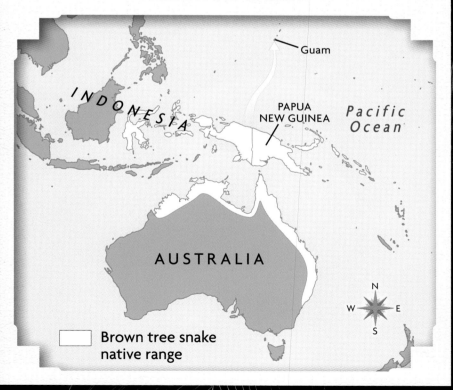

How Brown Tree Snakes Reached Guam

Guam

INDONESIA

PAPUA NEW GUINEA

Pacific Ocean

AUSTRALIA

N W E S

Brown tree snake native range

Guam is thousands of miles away from the countries where brown tree snakes are originally from.

So how did so many brown tree snakes end up on Guam? Scientists believe that in the 1940s a pregnant snake wriggled aboard a ship just before it headed to Guam from Papua New Guinea. At the trip's end, the snake slithered off the ship and found the ideal **habitat**. Guam was warm and wet, had many trees, and there were plenty of small animals for the snake to eat. Plus, there were no large predators.

The brown tree snake might have hitched a ride on a navy ship like this one.

There is only one snake that is native to Guam, and it's tiny and harmless.

A brown tree snake

Island Takeover

From just one **stowaway**, the brown tree snake population quickly grew. Female snakes can lay up to 12 eggs twice a year. After the babies hatched, there were no other snakes competing with the young brown tree snakes for food. As a result, lots of brown tree snakes survived to adulthood and had babies of their own.

A young brown tree snake

On Guam, brown tree snakes can grow as long as 9 feet (2.7 m).

The snakes scattered throughout the island, spreading about 1 mile (1.6 km) per year. In 20 years, the brown tree snake had reached nearly every corner of Guam. By 2014, there were more than one million snakes on the small island. That's about 5,000 snakes per square mile!

Much of Guam is covered with thick forests.

A photo of Guam taken from the sky

The New Boss

As the brown tree snake spread throughout Guam, it brought along its big appetite. The brown tree snake hunts mostly at night and can move quickly as it looks for prey. It slithers around in the dark, searching for eggs and animals such as birds, small lizards, rats, and mice to eat. Sometimes, the snake will even attack and gobble up dogs and other small pets!

A brown tree snake eats a lizard.

The brown tree snake can eat about 70 percent of its own weight during a meal. That's like an average-sized man eating 123 pounds (56 kg) of food at dinner!

When it finds its prey, the snake **lunges** forward to bite. Sharp fangs inside the snake's mouth release **venom** into the victim's body. That's not all, though. The snake then wraps its long body around its prey and squeezes, or constricts, the animal, causing it to stop breathing.

This brown tree snake searches for food.

fang

This photo, taken with a special microscope, shows a close-up view of a brown tree snake fang.

Gone Forever

Because the brown tree snake is such a great hunter and feeds often, it has wiped out many of Guam's **indigenous** animals. Birds have been especially hard hit. Since they have few ways of protecting themselves against the snake, ten out of eighteen birds native to the island are now gone.

The snakes also gobble down eggs and baby birds, which gives Guam's birds few chances to increase their numbers.

Brown tree snakes have killed all of the cardinal honeyeaters (shown above) on Guam.

A nest of birds' eggs

Birds are not the only victims. Five native lizards have also disappeared from Guam. In addition, small **mammals** called shrews have almost vanished. Soon, Guam's last native mammal—the Mariana fruit bat—could come close to disappearing, too.

Because brown tree snakes eat the young of Mariana fruit bats, the bats can no longer breed on Guam, which makes up a large part of their habitat.

The copper-striped blue-tailed skink is now gone from Guam thanks to the brown tree snake.

More Effects on Nature

With far fewer birds, Guam's **ecosystem** has changed. How? Birds feed on the seeds of certain kinds of trees. After they eat the seeds, the birds spread them around in their droppings. Now that so many of the birds are gone, very few of these seeds are spread. As a result, the forests have fewer of these seed-producing trees.

In this forest in Guam, no birds can be heard chirping.

An ecosystem is a group of animals and plants that depend on one another to survive. If one part of an ecosystem is destroyed, it has an effect on everything else.

The changes go beyond the trees. Guam's native birds ate many insects and spiders. Without the birds, the number of insects and spiders has **skyrocketed**. "You can't walk through the jungles on Guam without a stick in your hand to knock down the spiderwebs," says scientist Haldre Rogers. She and other scientists have found that there are now 40 times more spiders on Guam than on nearby islands.

Guam's forests are filled with huge spiderwebs such as this one.

One of Guam's many spiders

Snakes and People

Brown tree snakes don't just **inhabit** Guam's forests. As they search for food or places to rest, they have invaded houses and yards. People have found the snakes wriggling in their washing machines and barbeque grills and hanging from children's swing sets. The snakes have even been spotted in trash cans feeding on chicken wings!

Brown tree snakes have been found slithering in people's bathrooms.

The snakes sometimes crawl into homes at night and bite the people sleeping there. Although the snakes' venom is not harmful to adults, it can be dangerous to small children.

Some of the strangest spots the snakes crawl are into electrical boxes and onto power lines. When they do this, it damages the equipment. As a result, the animals have caused more than 1,200 power **outages** on Guam, which has had a big impact on the island's businesses. When the electricity goes out, shops and offices are forced to close until the power is fixed. Refrigerated food at supermarkets spoils. Experts say that the blackouts have cost Guam's businesses millions of dollars.

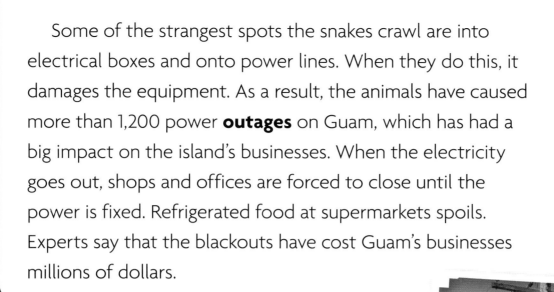

Brown tree snakes damage power lines.

This snake climbed over an electrical line and caused a power outage.

Fighting Back

The people of Guam are desperate to get rid of the snakes—or at least control their numbers. Government workers and scientists have tried many different methods to combat the invader. They have set up round wire traps to capture the snakes. So far, these traps have captured only a few thousand snakes per year.

A snake slithers into a round wire trap.
It can enter the trap but cannot get out of it.

People have also been testing some more unusual methods to control the snakes. That's where the parachuting mice come in. So far, using poisoned mice to kill the snakes is just a test. If the plan works, dead mice could be dropping out of the sky over Guam for a long time.

Using helicopters allows scientists to spread the dead mice over huge areas of Guam and kill more snakes.

tissue paper parachute

dead mouse

The dead mice are attached to tissue paper streamers that function as parachutes. The streamers are designed to get stuck on tree branches, where the snakes can easily find them.

No Exit

Finding ways to **eradicate** the brown tree snake is just one part of the problem. The other is making sure that snakes don't leave the island. Guam has busy **seaports** and airports. If a pregnant brown tree snake were to hitch a ride on another ship or plane, the same problem could start somewhere else.

Some brown tree snakes have already made it off the island. They have been found as far away as Texas and Oklahoma!

An airplane gets ready to leave Guam. Lots of goods move in and out of Guam on planes and ships.

Scientists and government workers have set hundreds of traps at Guam's seaports and airports to catch the reptiles. At night, spotlights shine brightly to frighten the snakes away from the **cargo**. Also, before each piece of cargo is loaded onto a plane or ship, it is carefully searched for hiding snakes. The snakes can twist their bodies into small spaces, so finding them can be a huge challenge.

Cargo is stored in big containers like these,
which snakes can easily wriggle into.

Sniffing for Snakes

Fortunately, government workers have brought in a helper to find snakes. It has four legs and a great sense of smell— the Jack Russell terrier. The U.S. government has gathered dozens of Jack Russells and sent them to Guam to help in the effort. The terriers are full of energy and determination and make great snake-**detection dogs**.

A Jack Russell terrier

Many of the Jack Russells used to sniff out snakes were rescued from shelters in the United States.

Once on the island, the terriers receive more than four months of special training on how to sniff out the brown tree snake. Then, after the dogs' training is complete, special **handlers** walk the terriers around planes and ships about to leave Guam. The dogs detect the snakes just by their smell. With the help of the terriers, a few hundred brown tree snakes were caught hiding at Guam's Andersen Air Force Base in 2012.

A U.S. Department of Agriculture employee works with a Jack Russell detection dog to search cargo for brown tree snakes.

Paradise Lost

One place that hopes to never see a brown tree snake is Hawaii. Like Guam, Hawaii has a tropical **climate** and lots of forests. Also, there are no predators there that could stop the spread of the snake. One Hawaiian scientist worried, "Once we get snakes here, we're never going to be able to fix the situation."

Hawaii is about 3,950 miles (6,357 km) east of Guam.

Native Hawaiian birds, such as this scarlet Hawaiian honeycreeper, could be in danger if brown tree snakes make their way to Hawaii.

Scientists are hopeful that the brown tree snake problem won't spread to Hawaii—or anywhere else. The fight to control these animals, however, is only just beginning. With millions of hungry snakes still slithering around Guam, it will take a huge effort to stop this animal invader.

Scientists are developing a **virus** that would kill brown tree snakes and not harm any other living things.

Other Invasive Reptiles

The brown tree snake is just one kind of reptile that has invaded Guam and the United States. Here are some others.

Black-and-White Tegu

- This lizard is native to South America but can now be found in Florida.

- The lizard can grow up to 4 feet (1.2 m) long.

- Tegus love to eat eggs, especially tortoise eggs. Scientists worry that the gopher tortoise—a turtle native to South Florida—may become **endangered** because of the tegu.

- On average, a female tegu can lay around 35 eggs per year.

Burmese Python

- The snakes are native to southern Asia and were first found in the Florida Everglades in the 1990s.

- The snake can grow to be more than 20 feet (6 m) long.

- Scientists believe there are thousands of these snakes slithering around Florida.

- These snakes have huge appetites, eating raccoons, opossums, and even bobcats and alligators!

Green Iguana

- The green iguana probably first came to the United States from Central America as a pet in the 1960s.

- Green iguanas eat plants and dig holes that can destroy special walls called dikes that are used to prevent flooding.

- When the weather gets cold, iguanas lose their grip on trees and can fall. This has been called a "frozen iguana shower."

Nile Monitor Lizard

- Nile monitors are a kind of lizard originally from Africa. They were first spotted in Florida in 1990 and have been found near Miami.

- They can grow up to 8 feet (2.4 m) long.

- These lizards have strong bodies and jaws that allow them to catch and eat almost anything smaller than they are.

- Nile monitor lizards are such fierce hunters that they are even known to attack the nests of Florida's native alligators.

Glossary

cargo (KAR-goh) goods carried by ship, airplane, or truck

climate (KLYE-mit) the typical weather in a place

detection dogs (di-TEKT-shuhn DAWGZ) types of dogs used to find things such as invasive animals, bombs, or drugs

ecosystem (EE-koh-*siss*-tuhm) a community of animals and plants that depend on one another to live

endangered (en-DAYN-jurd) in danger of dying out

eradicate (i-RAD-uh-kayt) to get rid of something completely

habitat (HAB-uh-*tat*) a place in nature where an animal lives

handlers (HAND-lurz) people who train and work with animals

hovers (HUHV-urz) stays in one place in the air

indigenous (in-DIJ-uh-nuhss) originating from a particular place

inhabit (in-HAB-it) to live in or occupy a place

invasive (in-VAY-siv) to spread all over and to cause harm

lunges (LUHNJ-iz) moves forward quickly and suddenly

mammals (MAM-uhlz) warm-blooded animals that have hair or fur and nurse their babies

native (NAY-tiv) being the place or environment in which an animal was born and originally lived

outages (OU-tij-uhz) power supply failures

parachutes (PA-ruh-*shoots*) lightweight fabric often attached to thin ropes that's used to slow the fall of something dropped out of an airplane or helicopter

population (pop-yuh-LAY-shuhn) the number of people or animals living in a place

predators (PRED-uh-turz) animals that hunt and kill other animals for food

reptiles (REP-tyelz) cold-blooded animals that have dry, scaly skin, such as snakes and lizards

seaports (SEE-ports) places where ships load and unload their goods

skyrocketed (SKYE-*rok*-it-id) to rise suddenly and quickly

stowaway (STOH-*uh*-way) a living thing that hides aboard a ship

toxic (TOK-sik) poisonous

tropical (TROP-i-kuhl) having to do with the warm areas of Earth near the equator

venom (VEN-uhm) poison that some animals, such as snakes, can send into the bodies of other animals through a bite or sting

virus (VYE-ruhss) a tiny germ that can be seen only with a powerful microscope; it can invade cells and cause disease

Bibliography

Jaffe, Mark. *And No Birds Sing: The Story of an Ecological Disaster in a Tropical Paradise.* New York: Simon & Schuster (1994).

Martin, Claire. "Where Have the Trees of Guam Gone?" *Smithsonian.com* (April 11, 2013).

Memmott, Mark. "Dead Mice Update: Tiny Assassins Dropped on Guam Again." NPR (December 3, 2013).

United States Department of Agriculture. *No Escape from Guam: Stopping the Spread of the Brown Tree Snake* (October 1998).

Read More

Bishop, Nic. *Snakes*. New York: Scholastic (2012).

Collard, Sneed B., III. *Science Warriors: The Battle Against Invasive Species (Scientists in the Field)*. Boston: Houghton Mifflin (2010).

Metz, Lorijo. *What Can We Do About Invasive Species? (Protecting Our Planet)*. New York: PowerKids Press (2010).

Learn More Online

To learn more about brown tree snakes and Guam, visit
www.bearportpublishing.com/TheyDontBelong

Index

About the Author

Kevin Blake lives in Providence, Rhode Island—far away from Guam and its millions of brown tree snakes—with his wife, Melissa, and son, Sam. This is his eighth book for kids.